THE WONDERFUL
WAY YOU ARE

Sarah Elizabeth Brooks

illustrations by
Sarah C. Dane

Download the free companion song and additional resources at
www.TheWonderfulWayYouAre.com

Copyright © 2020 by Sarah Elizabeth Brooks

All rights reserved. No portion of this book may be reproduced, stored in a retrieval system, or transmitted in any form or by any means—electronic, mechanical, photocopy, recording, scanning, or other—except for brief quotations in critical reviews or articles, without the prior written permission of the publisher.

Publisher's Cataloging-in-Publication Data

Names: Brooks, Sarah Elizabeth, author. Dane, Sarah C., illustrator.

Title: The Wonderful Way You Are: A Special Needs Picture Book / Sarah Elizabeth Brooks.

Summary: A rhyming picture book for children with special needs or disabilities.
Description: First edition. Clovis, NM: SEB Media, LLC, 2020.
Identifiers: LCCN 2020916345 | ISBN: Paperback 978-1-953550-00-2 | Hardcover 978-1-953550-01-9 | eBook 978-1-953550-02-6
Subjects: JUVENILE NONFICTION / Disabilities & Special Needs | Social Issues / Special Needs | Diversity & Multi-cultural | Social Themes -- Special Needs. BISAC: JNF053180.

Sarah Elizabeth Brooks's titles may be purchased in bulk for education, business, fund-raising, or sales promotional use. For quantity discount information, please e-mail Sales@Sarahebrooks.com.

Edited by Amy Parker
Author photo by Cristy Cross Photography

www.sarahebrooks.com

For
Ben, Andrew, James, and Elizabeth.
I love you through and through.

If you look at a snowflake,

You'll see they're not the same.

Like snowflakes, we're all different—

Different features,

different names.

The world may try to say that you
Should fit into its mold,
But sometimes being different means
At times you must be bold.

There may be days when you don't see yourself the way I do.
I think that you are special, and I love you through and through.

You might need hats and lotion to protect you from the sun,

Two wheels might take you places
So much faster than your feet.

You may need super-powered ears
To hear what others say.

But you must know I would not change
A single thing in you.

To some, your needs seem special–
But we're the same here deep inside.
Your path might be more rocky,
But I'm with you for the ride.

You may have days you wish you were like other girls and boys.
I wish that I could take your pain and leave you only joys.

The things that make you different mean
You stand out from the crowd.
We all can help each other find
A reason to feel proud.

It's true we all have struggles–every person here or there
Can sometimes use a helping hand,
To know somebody cares.

On rainy days when great big tears
Just cannot be held in,
I'll hold you close 'til storms have passed.
The sun will shine again.

the wonderful way you are

MEET THE KIDS FROM THE BOOK

Elizabeth, page 7

Elizabeth knows how to make sun-protective clothing look cool. She has Gorlin syndrome, which means she has to avoid UV rays, but that doesn't stop her from enjoying the outdoors with her three brothers. She loves unicorns and baby dolls. She's also a hydrocephalus warrior and has complete agenesis of the corpus callosum.

Micah, page 9

Micah J loves Jesus and wants to become a pastor when he grows up. His favorite activities are wrestling with his older brother, going to church, playing video games and having dinner with the family. In school he loves math and science and making friends. He has cerebral palsy and some of the coolest wheels in town.

Auburn, page 10

Auburn is a 9-year-old with cystic fibrosis who works hard daily to stay healthy by taking her medications, G-tube feedings, supplements, and treatments. Auburn loves dancing ballet, playing the violin, writing stories, reading adventure books, and spending time with friends and family.

Jake, page 13

Jake loves history, geography, quoting random trivia, and creating with Lego®. He loves to sing, especially worship songs, and wants to be an architect when he grows up. He loves every person he's ever met and gives the very best hugs. His superpower is autism.

Discussion Questions

1. What is your favorite thing about yourself?

2. Is there anything that is hard for you? How does that make you feel?

3. What is one thing you wish other people knew about you?

4. How can I help you on days when you feel sad or mad?

5. What is one way we can help others who may feel different?

Bonus Resources

Parents, sign up for our newsletter and receive a free downloadable PDF Activity Book featuring coloring pages, games, and a free mp3 download of the "Wonderful Way You Are" song.

Visit www.TheWonderfulWayYouAre.com to sign up.

If you are under 13, please ask permission from an adult before signing up.

Meet the Author

Sarah Elizabeth Brooks is a writer, indie musician, and special needs mom. When she's not writing or recording instrumental piano albums, you can find her dodging Mt. Laundry to sneak away with a cup of hot tea, some dark chocolate, and a good book.

She believes in the power of the written word, the beauty of community, and that every child deserves to see their story told.

Her daughter, Elizabeth, is the inspiration for this book.

Meet the Illustrator

Illustrator Sarah Dane is a California Baptist University Alumni and recently received her Masters of Fine Arts in Creative Writing from Saint Mary's College of California.

Aside from spending two years cartooning for a newspaper and her recent rise in social media attention, this book is her debut in illustration publication. According to her parents, Sarah has been drawing since she could hold a crayon.

@OLIVEDANEDRAWS

We don't have to say "Goodbye."

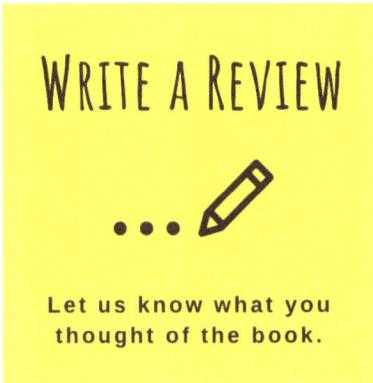

Write a Review

Let us know what you thought of the book.

Sharing is Caring

Share this book with a friend.

Stay in Touch

Connect with us online.

Did you enjoy the story?

Sarah would love to hear from you! Please leave a review at your favorite online retailer and let us know what you thought of the story. Tell us what you loved or how the book made you feel.

Share with a friend.

The biggest compliment you could give us would be sharing this book with a friend. If you share on social media, use #TheWonderfulWayYouAre so that we can say thank you!

Say hello!

Connect on Social Media:
@thesarahebrooks

Website:
www.sarahebrooks.com

E-mail:
Sarah@sarahebrooks.com

Sarah Elizabeth Brooks's titles may be purchased in bulk for education, business, fund-raising, or sales promotional use. Contact Sales@Sarahebrooks.com for information on quantity discounts.

For media inquiries or to schedule a school visit with the author, please contact: Media@Sarahebrooks.com.

If you are under 13, please ask an adult for permission before going online.

A big "Thank You" to these wonderful people who helped make this book possible:

Amy Barnett
Bjorklund Family
Chris Oaks
Ebrahim Al-Bishri
Gabriel, Isaiah & Gideon Bostwick
Jon, Ashley, and Jake Sumners
Judy Brooks
Kathy Koch

Landon Sammons
Lindsey Family
Loretta Heavyside
Michael Hopkins
Neil Aristy
Rachel, Gabrielle, & Megan Sloan
Stephen and Debbie Lowrie
Stephen Schilsky
Susie Barker
Tammy
Teena Hughes
Venita LaGrassa

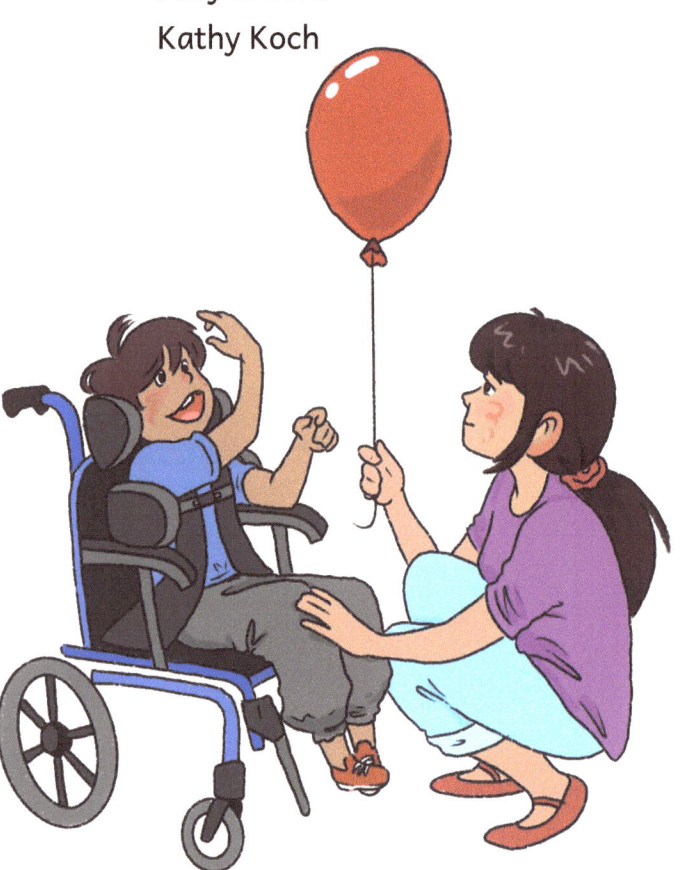

A special thank you to my husband, kids, and extended family for their support and encouragement as I've set out on this writing adventure.

I love you.
Sarah (aka Mom)

CPSIA information can be obtained
at www.ICGtesting.com
Printed in the USA
LVHW071106110121
676201LV00009B/274